STAY
POSITIVE
XOXO
Kim
Ann

# QUICK
# *Affirmations*
# FOR SUPER BUSY
# KIDS

## A TO Z OF EASY MOTIVATIONS
## FOR CREATING BETTER DAYS

### Kim Ann and Yobe Qiu

This book belongs to:

_____

# To Ruby,

Thank you for being an inspiration. Through your faith and confidence, you have overcome so many challenges. I admire your strength and your ability to remain positive and optimistic. I hope to follow your lead and become the best version of myself. Thank you for showing me how.

Love, Kim

# Quick Affirmations for Super Busy Kids

Are you ready to feel happier and more positive?

Sometimes, life can be challenging, and you might feel overwhelmed. When this happens, it's important to remind yourself how amazing you are. Focus on the good in your life, and remember what makes you special.

Reading positive affirmations can help you become more confident, resilient, and successful. When you believe in yourself and all that you can achieve, anything is possible!

That's why we created this A-to-Z affirmation collection. These affirmations are designed to help you let go of negativity and be your best self.

Read and recite the affirmations in this book every day. Remember that you are amazing, brilliant, and confident!

We hope this book helps you feel happy, healthy, and strong.

Happy reading!

Kim & Yobe

# I AM
## Appreciated,
### AND I KNOW
### THAT I'M
## Amazing!

# I AM
## Brave
### AND
## Brilliant!

I AM
Confident
IN MY
Choices.

I'M IN
Charge
OF ME!

I AM
Destined
FOR GREATNESS
AND Deserving
OF LOVE!

I Encourage AND Energize MYSELF AND MY FRIENDS!

# I AM
## Focused
### ON MY DAY!

I AM *Grateful* FOR ALL THAT I HAVE!

# I AM Helpful TO OTHERS!

I AM
Important,
AND I
Inspire
THE PEOPLE
AROUND ME!

# I HAVE Joy IN MY HEART!

I AM

# Kind

TO MYSELF AND

# Kind

TO OTHERS!

I AM
Loved
BY MANY!

# I AM

## Mindful

### OF THE
### WORLD AROUND ME!

# I AM Necessary AND Needed!

I AM
One-of-a-Kind,
AND I'M ALSO
Open Minded!

I AM
Proud
OF WHO I AM
AND WHAT I CAN DO!

I ASK IMPORTANT
AND NECESSARY
Questions!

I HAVE
Respect
FOR MYSELF
AND OTHERS!

I AM
Trustworthy
AND
Thoughtful!

I HAVE

Unique

IDEAS!

I HAVE
A GREAT Vision
OF WHERE I
WANT TO BE!

# I AM
# Wonderful
## AND Worthy!

XOXO

I SEND
*Hugs* AND *Kisses*
TO MY FAMILY,
MY FRIENDS, AND
THE WHOLE WORLD!

# Yes!

## I CAN MAKE
## A DIFFERENCE!

I AM
Zen,
AND I CAN
FIND PEACE!

ZEN TRUSTWORTHY One-of-a-Kind Needed

Joy Wonderful SMART

THOUGHTFUL Amazing Grateful Inspire Brave APPRECIATED

YES Mindful

QUESTIONS

Charge Confident DESTINED

Deserving

WORTHY Helpful RESPECT

NECESSARY

Kind Brilliant ENCOURAGE

SUCCESSFUL Unique OPEN Loved

XOXO MINDED

ENERGIZE Important

CHOICES VISION

PROUD Focused

# Affirmations

_____

_____

_____

_____

_____

_____

_____

_____

_____

_____

_____

_____

_____

_____

# Affirmations

_____

_____

_____

_____

_____

_____

_____

_____

_____

_____

_____

_____

_____

# OTHER BOOK TITLES IN THE
## Quick Affirmations Series

AFFIRMATION CARDS AND MERCHANDISE AVAILABLE

# luckyfourpress.com
## #QuickAffirmations

CPSIA information can be obtained
at www.ICGtesting.com
Printed in the USA
JSHW041105290722
28699JS00003B/110

9 781953 774293